DISNEY'S ELEGANT ABC BOOK

By Vincent Jefferds

Includes special sections on Letter Construction and Numbers 1 to 10

Little Simon
Published by Simon & Schuster, New York

Published by LITTLE SIMON, a Simon & Schuster Division of Gulf & Western Corporation.
Simon & Schuster Building, 1230 Avenue of the Americas, New York, New York 10020.
LITTLE SIMON and colophon are trademarks of Simon & Schuster. Printed in the United States of America.
10 9 8 7 6 5 4 3 2 1
ISBN: 0-671-45571-0

A

A is for artist,
With smock and beret.
He's all covered with paint
By the end of the day.

A is for ape.

I saw some apes down at the zoo,
    And then I saw some monkeys, too.
The monkeys use their tails to hang,

But not the poor orangutang.
Each time he tries this trick, he fails—
    Because the apes do not have tails.

I overheard one big ape say,
    "Sure tails are cute,
But they get in the way."

A is for apple,
And Alice, too.
She has one for herself,

And one for you.

B

B is for Bambi.
  He's puzzled — know why?
He's just turned and seen
  His first butterfly.

B is for brother.
  If you have one, who needs another?
But if you have none,
  One might be fun!

B is for bump,
  You can see how it's growing.
This won't happen to you,
  If you look where you're going.

B is for bee,
    But remember one thing.
The front is all honey,
    But the back is all sting.

C is for Cinderella.

A coach from a pumpkin,
 A gown, and glass shoe;
Her godmother made
 All her wishes come true.

C is for cow.

She munches on grass,
    And she chews it, my friend,

And then we get milk
From the cow's other end.

C is for cat,
    With hair soft as silk.
He'll stay nice and fat,
    If he drinks lots of milk.

D

D is for Dumbo,
   Who flew without fears,
Thanks to the help of
   His extra-big ears.

D is for dig.
   See Pluto alone?
He thinks no one's watching
   Him bury his bone.

D is for Donald,
    A hot-tempered duck.

You would be too,
    If you had his bad luck!

E is for eyes.

Your eyes take pictures all day long,
And some your mind will keep.

But most of them will disappear,
When once you fall asleep.

E is for ear.
Rest your eyes on this setter.
He can hear with one ear,
But two are much better.

E is for eggs,
With most of them matching,

Except in this case,
Where one is just hatching!

E is for Eeyore.

Eeyore's short and gray and grumpy,
  Stuffed with straw that's dry and lumpy.
Another thing that makes him cross—
  His tail comes off. That's quite a loss.

F

F is for fall.
(Ball has the
same sound.)

If you fall you are flat;
    If a ball—you are round.

F is for fun.

If you like picnics in the sun,
And feel content when day is done.

If you can laugh and play and run,
I'd say you're having lots of fun.

F is for feathers.

Birds all have feathers
    To help them to fly.
In cold and wet weather,
    They help keep them dry.

G is for goat.

Do you see Mr. Goat?
 Here he's strolling and strutting.
If you don't make him mad,
 There's no if, and, or butting.

G is for Goofy.

Goofy is a happy guy.

He'll give anything a try.

Winds up looking
such a sight,

Because he just can't
do things right.

H

H is for hope.
It's a trait that we share
With the whole human race
In the world everywhere.

H is for Hook.

Hook was a Captain of old pirate fame.
   Would you like to know how he got his strange name?
The people all viewed him with fright and alarm—
   He had a sharp hook at the end of his arm.

H is for hair.

Hair always grows
    On the top of your head.
What if it grew
    On your feet instead?

I is for Indian.

Indians roamed the woods and plain,
And lived in peace; then others came.
These people took their land away.
The Indians' loss is our own today.

I is for Ichabod, Ichabod Crane.
　　After Halloween night, he was never the same.
Folks around here most often say,
　　"A pumpkin-head figure scared him away."

J

Do you see the jet trail
In the sky?
It's the fastest plane
That you can fly.

J is for jump.
  See Goofy up there?
He's using his legs
  To jump in the air.

J is for Jaq.

Jaq was a mouse,
    A fine little fellow.
In spite of his size,
    He saved Cinderella.

K

K is for kicks.
   When you're walking alone,
Sometimes it's fun
   To kick a loose stone.

K is for kite

When your kite's in the air,
Hold the string very tight,

Or soon you will find
That it's way out of sight.

L is for love.
And in all kinds of weather,
For family and friends,
It will go on forever.

L is for ladder,
The tallest in town.
It was fun going up;
I was scared coming down.

L is for leg,
    That part of you
That eventually runs
    Into your shoe.

M is for mother,
   Who knows just what to do.
Haven't you been lucky?
   God made one just for you.

M is for Mickey,
  A lovable mouse.
I'm sure that quite often
  He visits your house.
In comics and games,
  And I'm sure that you see

Mickey's red pants on your color TV.

M is for monsters.

Make-believe monsters
In movies and books,
Make everyone jump
With their frightening looks.

But those make-believe monsters
Would run away fast,
If they saw a real monster
From out of the past!

N

N is for nose,
    It sticks out of your face.
Put your hand on it now,
    Is it in the right place?

N is for numbers.

When you learn how to use them,
    You'll really be glad.
Count your toes and your fingers,
    Subtract and then add.

O is for orange.

You can't swallow an orange
　　To get out the juice.
Ask this dumb ostrich,
　　"What's your excuse?"

O is for ostrich.
   A bird that can't sing.
And he can't even fly
   With such a small wing.

P

P is for Pinocchio.

Pinocchio was made of wood,
　　But when he learned how to be good,
To Geppetto's pride and joy,
　　He turned into a real, live boy.

P is for Pooh,
    Who needs love and care.
He's not very smart,
    He's just a stuffed bear.

P is for pencil.

A pencil is only
    As smart as you.
It will do whatever
    You tell it to.

P is for pigs.

This is a story of three little pigs
Who were chased by a big, bad wolf.

He tried every way to catch them at play,
But finally he climbed on their roof.

Down the chimney, the bad wolf climbed.
   But a hot water pot
Is what the wolf got.
   And he quickly changed his mind.

Q is for quiet,
When your friends all around
Are not singing or talking
Or making a sound.

Q is for the Queen of Hearts.

Alice could not stand the Queen.
    The Queen was rude and very mean—
The meanest thing you've ever seen,
    With a head shaped like a kidney bean.
She chased Alice most of the day,
    But Alice finally got away.

R is for right,
 Which can be a direction,
But also implies
 A sense of perfection.

R is for run,
A trick you can master.

It's like when you walk,
But your legs move much faster.

R is for Robin Hood.
  He made a switch,
'Cause he gave to the poor
  What he took from the rich.

S is for saw.

Using a saw
   Looks like fun.
It makes two pieces
   Out of one.

S is for snow.

When you're thirsty,
Snow tastes nice,
Because it's little
Flakes of ice.

S is for Snow White.

Snow White lived with
   The seven dwarfs,
To hide from the wicked queen,
   Of course.

S is for Scrooge.

His nickels are much,
And his dollars many.
But he isn't likely
To give you any.

S is for scary.

The witch was so scary!
She followed Snow White,
But don't be upset now—
Things turn out all right.

T

T is for television.

Your use of it
   Will start receding,
As you learn
   The joy of reading.

T is for trunk.
   That's on Dumbo, and see—
Here's a trunk you can pack,
   And a trunk of a tree.

T is for teeth.

Brush after meals,
   Not just once in a while.
Then people will say,
   "What a beautiful smile."

T is for tiger,
   A giant striped cat.
If you go in the jungle,
   Avoid where he's at.

U

U is for up,
   Where the sky is all blue.
But looking ahead
   Is important, too.

U is for under.

See friend duck,
   Swinging free,
Enjoying himself
   Under a tree.

U is for Uncle Remus.

Uncle Remus lived in the wood,
   And the children would visit
whenever they could.

Telling the tales of Brer Fox and Brer Rabbit
   Was Uncle Remus's lovable habit.

V is for vegetables
That grow row on row.
You just plant the seeds,
And then watch them grow!

V is for Vincent.
Now take a quick look.
You'll find it's my name
On the front of your book.

V is for vine,
A plant that has fun
Creeping and crawling
Up towards the sun.

BEANS

W

W is for wait.

"Wait" is a word that means "not now,"
So you might prefer to miss this.
But a little patience will surely help,
When it gets close to Christmas.

W is for window.

A window lets in
   The fresh air and light,
And a view of the moon
   On a beautiful night.

W is for witches.

Witches are a kind of fairy,
   But they're mean and sometimes scary.

W is for wheel.

On cars and trains and bikes it's fair
  To say it's wheels that get you there.
They'd never work if they were square!

X

X is for xylophone,
 To fit in this rhyme.
But you won't need this word
 Till you're going on nine.

X is for X-ray.

When an X-ray looks at your inside,
There's nothing much you can hide.

Y

Y is for yo-yo.

A yo-yo is an amazing thing,
    It spins up and down as you pull on a string.

Y is for yell.
   It sounds the same,
If you're calling for help
   Or howling in pain!

Z is for zebra,
Who has a striped hide.
Look at him here,
Giving Goofy a ride.

Z is for zero.

Play in the house
   When it's zero degrees.
If you go out-of-doors,
   You will certainly freeze.

Get some paper and a pencil or crayon, we're going to have fun making some letters.

I is the alphabet's hero,
  Its great and shining star.
It makes so many letters,
  If you add a curve or bar.

Curves are half circles,

Bars can be up or down.

Here's an easy one for you to see—

Cross the with a bar

and it makes a

If you've done that,
You're doing well.
Put a bar at the bottom,

And make an L.

Add two bars,
And what do we see?
You have made yourself

A capital E.

LOVE

If you drop the bottom bar,
F is the letter—there you are!

I can be used in another way.

Add a curve at the end,

And you'll make a J.

Put two curves together,
And take a guess.

You have made
A capital S.

S

H is like a jumping star—
He needs two I's with a crossing bar.

We're having too much fun to stop.

Squeeze your H together at the top.

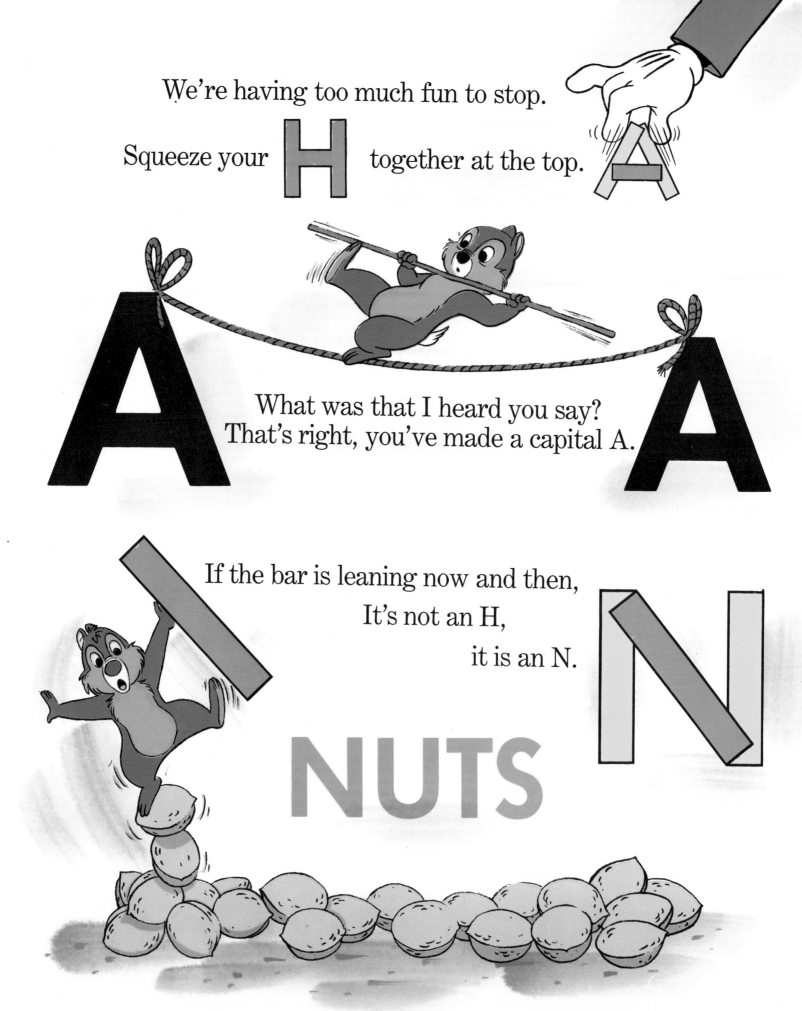

What was that I heard you say?
That's right, you've made a capital A.

If the bar is leaning now and then,
It's not an H,

it is an N.

NUTS

Let's try something harder.
Now this is a gem—

Put a V with two I's,
And you'll then have an M.

MOW

Some letters like to play the clown.
W is an M upside down.

V is another
    That likes to clown.
V is two bars pointing down.

The V can be changed,
    So give it a try.
Add one bar,
    And it makes a Y.

Lay a V on its side, And add to the I,

And you've made a K
    On your very first try.

KEY

AN INTRODUCTION TO THE NUMBERS

1 is fine for me and you,
But for a shoe,
Only **2** will do.

If peanuts are free,
I'll take **3**.

Or maybe **4** —
4 is more.

Look at the bees
Fly from the hive.
I counted **5**.

I'd be in a fix,
If I said **6**.

But here are **6** ants,
 Crawling up Donald's pants.
Before he's awake,
 They may eat all his cake.

Dwarfs are small,
  But oh, good heavens!
Must they always
  Come in sevens?

The hands on the clock
  Point to **8**.
My goodness
  It is getting late!

Things are never what they seem.
I saw **9** heffalumps in a dream.

One flower's charming in its way,
But **10** will make a nice bouquet.